Finding ʻOli

A True Love Story About A
Critically Endangered Hawksbill Sea Turtle

Marjorie Tyler

Finding 'Oli
A True Love Story About A Critically Endangered Hawksbill Sea Turtle

Copyright © 2020 Marjorie Tyler

ISBN: 978-1-7356932-0-0
ISBN: 1-7356932-0-0
Library of Congress Control Number: 2020938840

Cover and all painted images by Marjorie Tyler
Photos provided by Cheryl King and Anita Wintner
Cover design by Vanimdesign.com

Sacred Life Publishers™
SacredLife.com

Printed in the United States of America

"Are you going to Big Beach tomorrow to look for a turtle's nest?" Anita asked. Her mother took a last sip of coffee and looked up from the morning paper. "You know I go every Tuesday morning."

"Oh, please, Mama," Anita begged. "Please can I come with you? I am *almost* five years old!" Her mother paused as she carried the breakfast dishes to the sink. "Yes, Anita," she replied with a smile. "I think this year you are ready to join Dawn Patrol."

"Really? Oh, Mama!" Anita wrapped her small arms around her mother's waist and then twirled around the kitchen in a dance of joy.

Early the next morning, Anita and her mother set out through the deep woods that lay between their home and the beach. They heard the loud thunder of the waves crashing on the sand. Anita wondered how a turtle could brave such powerful waves, crawl up out of the sea and across the wide beach to find a safe nesting place among the sand dunes.

As they came out of the woods, they had their first view of Big Beach and the brilliant, blue ocean beyond. Anita's mother stopped suddenly, and Anita looked up in surprise.

"Look, Anita! Do you see those markings in the sand?" she asked and pointed toward the water.

Anita followed her mother's pointing finger, and her eyes widened. All the way from the water's edge, across the beach and up to the trees, were what looked like deep tire tracks left by an enormous truck. A second set of tracks returned to the sea. "A hawksbill turtle made those tracks, Anita," her mother whispered, eyes sparkling. "We have a new nest!"

A mother turtle had returned during the night to this beach, where she had been born maybe twenty-five years before. She chose a cool place covered by the shade of giant kiawe trees, far enough away from the changing tides that the nest would stay safe and dry. With her powerful flippers she dug through two feet of sand to lay her soft-shelled eggs. They would hatch in about sixty days.

Anita skipped happily over the sand. Her mother made a careful note of just where the turtle's nest lay. "You have been my good luck charm today, Anita!" she exclaimed, drawing Anita into a warm hug.

They finished walking the rest of the beach to make sure there weren't more tracks, which was highly unlikely since hawksbill nests are rare. They were lucky the turtle chose last night to lay her eggs so Anita and her mother could discover the tracks from the first nest of the season today. All the way home they talked about turtles, turtles, turtles!

Anita's mother explained that the mother turtle will find a spot somewhere on the reef to rest while her new batch of eggs (sometimes over 200) develop inside her. Then she will swim back to the Big Beach area in another two-to-three weeks to crawl ashore bravely and lay a new nest. She'll probably repeat that for a total of five nests this summer! Then she will swim all the way back to where she lived when she wasn't on her nesting mission. That might be on a different island!

"I know you haven't learned much math yet, Anita, but you will. If we have five nests with 200 eggs in each of them, that could mean that we get to watch over 1,000 hatchlings this season!" Anita was just so excited to get to see one hatchling! Two months sure was a long time to wait.

Anita thought of that first new nest as her very own. Her mother promised that they would sleep out on the beach, next to the nest, at hatching time with their good friend, Cheryl, a marine biologist. She worked for an organization that studies and protects hawksbill turtles. Cheryl and her dedicated volunteers have spent many days and nights on Big Beach searching for nesters, and then watching for the little hatchlings to appear to make sure they all crawl to the ocean safely. Anita wanted to help as much as possible this summer.

"What do you call someone who knows all about turtles?" Anita asked. She was sitting on the couch with her father. He was reading the newspaper and she was looking at her favorite book of pictures of sea creatures. "Hmm," her father looked puzzled. "I don't know, Anita. But a turtle is a marine reptile, and someone who studies reptiles is called a herpetologist, I think."

"That's what I'm going to be when I grow up," Anita declared. "A marine herpetologist."

"A fine ambition," her father replied.

The summer days tumbled by, and Anita managed to tuck thoughts of the turtle nest to the back of her mind until bedtime. Then, she would look at her tidy bundle—sleeping bag, sweatshirt, red flashlight—waiting beside the bedroom door, and feel a shiver of anticipation.

"Today is the day, Anita," her mother announced. "Gather your things together. Tonight, we camp on Big Beach!"

Anita, her mother, and Cheryl prepared their chairs and sleeping bags on the sand near the turtle's nest. They would take turns through the night, sleeping and watching quietly.

Cheryl explained to Anita, "We can only loosely predict when the turtles will emerge by our past experiences with the nests. We just have to be patient. It's all about the temperature: the hotter the nest is, the faster they incubate. And, that means there will likely be more female hatchlings. Then, it can take days to wiggle out of their eggshells and crawl out of their sandy nest to the surface."

Anita couldn't believe they could breathe and move under all of that sand. She was worried about them and wanted to dig them out, but knew they had to let nature take its course. The turtles would find a way.

Lulled by the lapping of the waves and the soft evening breeze, Anita drifted off to sleep. She was swimming with the turtles in a dreamy haze when she was awakened by her mother's gentle nudge. "The turtles are here!"

Anita sat up and rubbed her eyes. One after another, the tiny brown heads popped up through the sand. A flurry of miniature flippers followed. The baby turtles were greeting the world for the first time under the light of a full moon. They headed straight for the water. How did they know which way to go? Anita stood up and gazed in amazement. Cheryl and her mother shooed the hungry ghost crabs away. Marching over mounds of sand, toppling over and struggling to control those brand-new flippers, they reached the waves and were swept into their new, watery world.

Anita had fallen in love. She made a wish upon a star that night that she would find one of those special turtles again one day.

Anita would have to become a good swimmer and learn to snorkel before she could begin her search for the turtles. She was in the water every chance she could get! She knew in her heart that her wish would someday come true. Her parents watched, amazed at how hard she was willing to work.

For her fifth birthday, she received a wonderful present. Her parents gave her a special camera designed to take pictures both on land and under water. Anita was thrilled! They also gave her a large scrapbook, and that very day she started a collection of ocean scenes and sea life. It became a beautiful book. She and her friends spent hours taking pictures of shells and other treasures on the beach. Her teacher was especially pleased when she brought the photographs to school for show and tell.

Anita believed that Maui was a magical place. Sunrise brought schools of playful dolphins, leaping from the water, and spinning in midair. Wherever she went on the island, the air carried the sweet smells of tropical flowers. At sunset, the sky glowed with bands of glorious color. And all around her, in all seasons, the blue ocean beckoned.

The whales came in the wintertime, swimming from the cold waters of Alaska to the warm waters of Hawai'i. Here, their babies were born. Anita watched the pods cruise through the waves. Sparkling fountains were tossed upward as the whales breathed through their blowholes. When she went snorkeling in whale season, she could hear the songs of the males from miles away—mooing, clicking, and cooing.

Summertime brought the freedom of school-less days. Then the ocean became her whole world, and she delighted in the beautiful, strange, and whimsical creatures she found there.

The summer Anita was ten would prove to be the most eventful summer of her life. She had become a strong swimmer and now snorkeled out to the farthest reaches of the reef. She often went out with her "snorkel buddy" Auntie Maile, who loved the waters around Maui as much as Anita did.

Sunlight slanting through the water lit up the reef in dazzling colors. They played peek-a-boo with the striped sergeant fish, followed schools of the silvery, whiskered goatfish, watched the octopus change colors and the eels slide in and out of their caves. Together they explored much of the reef near her home, and Anita shared with Auntie Maile her secret wish to find a hawksbill turtle. Big green turtles, *honu*, were often eating seaweed close to the shore. But day after day, no hawksbill, *honu'ea* appeared.

One calm morning, Anita and her mother decided to venture out to a part of the reef they had not yet explored. They slipped into the water. The shimmering, blue-green world welcomed them, and they glided over the reef, gazing in all directions. Anita couldn't believe her eyes! Swimming right in front of them was a young hawksbill turtle! It was the smallest turtle Anita had ever seen swimming in the ocean. It was also the most beautiful! It was her wish come true.

Anita wanted to shout for joy! She swam cautiously toward the turtle and, to her delight, it turned to face her as if to say, *"Aloha."* Anita knew in her heart that they would be friends. The perfect name came to her. She would call her 'Oli, which means "joy" in Hawaiian. The turtle dove down to the ocean bottom and wedged herself under a ledge of coral to take a nap.

Anita's mother could see in her daughter's face that she had truly found *joy!* Back on shore, however, she offered words of caution. "Now you must be very careful with 'Oli," she said. "Of course, you will be friends, but you must watch and learn from her. Make sure you give her plenty of room to swim and play, and you must never try to touch her." Anita knew all these things and promised that she would never do anything to harm 'Oli.

She looked for 'Oli every day. When she woke up in the morning, her first thoughts were of 'Oli. She leapt out of bed, hoping always for clear weather and smooth waters. And most summer days Anita did find 'Oli, close to her coral home, playing hide-and-seek with the big honu. Sometimes Anita didn't have to look for her at all. 'Oli just appeared—gliding, dipping, drifting toward her.

They loved swimming together, Anita bobbing up with 'Oli from time to time as she took a breath of air at the surface. "Mirroring" was the most fun! Right flipper, right arm. Left flipper, left arm. Anita kept time with 'Oli, who swam a few feet below her. The happy summer sped by. Anita had never been so excited!

She was running down to the beach, her eyes already scanning the waves, planning another day with 'Oli. *Whoops! Kerplunk!* Her feet went out from under her, and she fell flat on her stomach. Her leg! A stab of pain. She hardly dared to look. A stream of blood was flowing from a deep cut just below her knee. She slowly raised herself up. Right behind her a sharp tip of lava rock peered out of the sand. She squeezed her eyes shut against the pain and could just hear her parents' frequent warnings, "Watch where you're going! Slow down! Pay attention to the hidden lava rock!"

Anita hobbled home and called out to her mother.

"Anita! What on earth has happened to you?" her mother cried in alarm. Anita could hardly answer. One look at her daughter's face and the blood running down her leg, and her mother knew that a trip to the emergency room was called for. She wrapped a clean towel around the cut, bundled Anita into the car, and off they sped.

The ER doctors and nurses were kind and efficient. They quickly cleaned the wound and stitched it up. Anita was just feeling the beginnings of relief when the terrible news came. "You'll have to stay out of the water until this has completely healed," the doctor told her sternly. "Ocean water contains bacteria that can cause serious infections."

"How long will that be?" she asked in a small voice. "I'm afraid it might be as long as a month," the doctor answered. She leaned against her mother and hid her face. A whole month without 'Oli! How would she bear it?

It was a sad and silent ride home. Anita climbed out of the car and said, "I'm going down to the beach." Her mother said nothing but let her go. Anita sat on the sand, gazing out toward the reef, thinking of her friend. She decided to look for trash to clean up, which made her feel better since that would help all of her ocean friends.

She was almost dizzy with excitement when the doctor finally gave her permission to get back in the water. She ached with the missing of 'Oli. The next day, she and her mother swam out to the reef. Anita's head danced with questions, "Will she be here? Will she remember me?"

Anita's eyes scanned the crevices and outcroppings of coral, and there she was, her 'Oli! But as they got closer, they noticed that something was terribly wrong. 'Oli did not come up to greet them as usual. Anita and her mother looked at each other through their masks, asking silently, "Do you see what I see? Can this really be happening to the one we love?"

On the side of 'Oli's neck was a huge lump, almost as big as a golf ball. It was big enough to make it difficult for her to move her neck! What had happened? What could they do to help? Her mother signaled to her to turn back, and with broken hearts they returned to shore. Slipping into their flip-flops, anxious and confused, they rushed home. Anita was fighting back tears. Her mother was quiet, thinking of the best way to save her daughter's precious friend.

As soon as she walked in the door, Anita's mother was on the phone to Cheryl, hoping she would know what to do. Cheryl was immediately ready to help. She knew a scientist in Honolulu, on the island of O'ahu, who could advise them. "Let's call our friend George at the National Oceanic and Atmospheric Administration (NOAA), since we worked with him to tag 'Oli. He'll remember, and he knows how endangered hawksbills are, so every single one is extremely important! I'll get back to you as soon as I can."

Anita wondered if such a busy man who has tagged so many turtles would be interested in one sick, little hawksbill. She learned a lot on that tagging research day, especially how much adults cared about turtles and the ocean. She never knew sea turtles got the same tiny tags as pet dogs and cats. And measuring 'Oli confirmed just how small she was: her shell measured 38.5 cm long and she only weighed 11.5 pounds!

To find out more about them, the biologists also caught some honu and two other hawksbills that day (who had the names #MUI-11 "The Turtle Formerly Known as Prince" and #MUI-15 "Hope"), who were much bigger than 'Oli. As Cheryl had explained before, George also told Anita that 'Oli was too small to tell whether it was a boy or a girl (they have to be adult size, twice as big as 'Oli is now), but Anita always thought of 'Oli as a joyful girl. "Her" scientific number in Cheryl's photo-ID database is #MUI-27.

Anita also remembered all of the fishing line and hooks they cleaned up off the reef that day. Is that what happened to 'Oli's neck? Or was it something that 'Oli ate? Did she have a disease? Or what? There are so many dangers in the ocean 'Oli has to survive every day! Would they ever know the truth?

Cheryl called back moments later. "George has given me permission to examine 'Oli," she said with excitement. "Then I'll report back to him, and we'll take it from there. Let's go out tomorrow morning!"

The next day, Cheryl and her boyfriend, Jake, met Anita on the beach. They were so kind and so interested in helping ʻOli. They swam quickly out to the reef. Anita led Cheryl right to ʻOli's spot, and there she was, sadly hiding under the coral. The sparkle had disappeared from her half-closed eyes. The lump on her neck looked even bigger now than it had yesterday.

Carefully, Cheryl dove down to ʻOli's resting place and reached out her hand to ʻOli's neck. The sick turtle seemed to welcome Cheryl's gentle touch. She made no attempt to swim away. She slowly brought ʻOli to the surface to have a better look . . . . The lump was something Cheryl hadn't seen before in all the turtles she knew.

Back on shore, Cheryl contacted George and talked with him about what could be done. Anita saw the concern on Cheryl's face and became even more frightened. Cheryl turned to her and said, "Try not to worry too much, Anita. It is because of your love for 'Oli that she is now going to get the help she needs. Have hope!"

George came up with a plan. He would fly to Maui himself, then they would swim out to find and catch 'Oli. In a special carrier, 'Oli would fly to Honolulu, where George had arranged to have her examined by another turtle specialist, a veterinarian. It seemed like an impossible dream. But now there was reason to hope!

At the appointed time, George arrived with a large dog carrier and snorkel gear. They had called on Auntie Maile and other friends to help in the search and rescue mission.

The sea was treacherous that morning! Enormous waves churned the sand and visibility was near zero. "Oh, Anita," her mother said with a sigh of dismay, "I can't let you go out in this. You're not strong enough. And your leg is only just healed."

"Mama!" Anita cried, "'Oli will die if we don't find her today!"

"I'm afraid your mother's right, Anita," Cheryl said. "We can't worry about losing you, too. With all of us searching, I know we will find her."

Anita stood looking down at her sandy feet, unwilling to yield.

"Anita," Cheryl continued, "we're not only helping 'Oli. Countless other turtles may benefit from what the veterinarians learn from her. Your 'Oli is a very special sea turtle. We will find her."

Anita's disappointment was eased somewhat by a swelling of pride. 'Oli had become the most cherished thing in her own life. And now 'Oli would be an important part of many other lives as well.

"Let's go!" George called. The searchers plunged into the wild waters. The waves were so high; it would be all but impossible for them to signal to one another. They searched and searched. Precious time was passing, and hope was fading. Anita, waiting anxiously on shore, feared that this one chance for 'Oli's rescue would fail.

Suddenly, a turtle's head bobbed over the top of a wave! It was coming toward shore. Anita had never seen 'Oli venture so close to the shoreline, but hope surged within her. She waved and pointed and called out. Cheryl saw her signal and managed to catch a glimpse of the turtle. It *was* 'Oli. It was a miracle! 'Oli was making it easy for her rescuers, as if she understood that they had come to help her.

George also saw the turtle and swam toward her. He reached through the murky water and felt for the back of 'Oli's shell. Wrapping his strong arms around 'Oli, he felt the frightened turtle nestle into his chest. Without a struggle, they swam to shore.

The crowd on the beach cheered! Anita blinked back tears of joy. Cheryl and the others came scrambling back onto the beach, exhausted but exuberant.

Not wanting to waste time, George carefully placed ʻOli in her carrier and thanked everyone on the beach. Anita tried to imagine what ʻOli must be feeling—out of the water, all these strangers, locked in a cage. But things were happening so quickly. George had placed ʻOli in his car and, with a final wave, they were off to Kahului airport and their flight to Honolulu.

George had promised to return in five days. Five days! It felt like an eternity to Anita. She tossed and turned in her bed all night. Nightmare visions swam before her eyes of a frightened little turtle, all alone, yearning for the water. Her worst fear was that she might never see 'Oli again.

And then came the good news. George called to report the veterinarian's findings. 'Oli would be fine! She had a large abscess on her neck, which the doctor had drained. He placed her on antibiotics, and he expected her to fully recover. Anita felt a relief beyond words.

But there was *more* thrilling news: Anita learned that 'Oli was probably around six years old. Anita had been almost five when she saw those first baby turtles leave their nest. Now she was almost eleven. Six years older! She was certain that 'Oli was one of the turtles she had seen march down to the ocean on that moonlit night. Her wish *had* come true!

Tingling with excitement, Anita waited, straining to see the first sign of an approaching car. It had been five agonizing days. Her mother, Cheryl, and Jake stood with her. Cheryl smiled at Anita in her eagerness. "Not long now, Anita. 'Oli will soon be home."

At last George appeared, carrier in hand. Glynnis, Steve, and Esten, with the United States Fish and Wildlife Service (USFWS) Dawn Patrol, were also there to help. Anita ran to greet her beloved turtle. 'Oli's neck was almost back to its normal size, but her shell looked so dry. Anita could hardly wait to see her returned to the ocean where she belonged.

Steve placed 'Oli gently on the waves and they all swam a little way alongside her. 'Oli looked around in a puzzled way, trying to get her bearings. Anita held her breath. Under water, her mother gave her hand an encouraging squeeze. The suspense was beginning to tie a knot in Anita's stomach, when all of a sudden, flippers prepared for takeoff—and *whoosh!* 'Oli jetted toward the open sea! Anita had never seen a turtle swim so fast. 'Oli was home! As they bobbed to the surface, they clapped and cheered, sharing in 'Oli's joy.

Feeling the familiar waters embrace her body and soothe away the dry scales that covered her shell, 'Oli said her own turtle prayer of thanks. Her frightening adventure was fading like a troubled dream. But she had seen that the world was a much bigger place than she could have imagined, and she felt the wonder of it. 'Oli sped out into the sunlit waters—farther out than she had ever been before. A new, exciting life awaited her.

Days passed. Anita returned again and again to the reef, but she could not find 'Oli. For the hundredth time, she asked her mother, "Do you think 'Oli is okay? How will we know if she really survived?"

"We just have to have faith, and hope for the best," her mother replied, knowing that this was not the assurance Anita was hoping to hear.

Anita called on her friends to help. Everyone on the beach was given a description of the little hawksbill turtle. Anita, Cheryl, and her Turtle Team spent hours at a time in the ocean, hoping to find 'Oli.

And then one morning, when summer was almost over, Anita woke with a new feeling of certainty. "This will be the day. Today I will find 'Oli!" She hurried down to the beach. Where to look first? Anita and her wonderful Auntie Maile looked in all the usual places, but no 'Oli. They swam farther out than they had ever been before. Their eyes searched the dip and rise of every wave, each nook and cranny of the reef below.

Suddenly, there was a little hawksbill, swimming not far away! It moved gracefully, sweeping back and forth around heads of coral and through schools of colorful fish. Could it possibly be—yes! It was 'Oli! Anita's heart burst with delight. 'Oli swam to her and seemed to say, "I have missed you, too, but I've been on a wonderful journey."

Epilogue

Fifteen years later, under the light of a full moon, a turtle named 'Oli is carried to shore on a gentle wave. She is returning to Big Beach on the island of Maui where she was born, where her mother was born, where her babies will be born. With her powerful flippers, she makes her way across the sand to the shade of the kiawe trees, digs her nest, and lays her eggs. Then she covers the nest with sand and returns to the sea.

The following morning at dawn, a young woman named Anita steps out of the deep woods onto the beach and sees the clear, familiar markings in the sand. She makes a careful note of the location of the new nest. At the appointed time, she will return with a few friends to wait and to watch as these hatchlings greet the world for the first time.

More Information about Hawksbill Turtles

The hawksbill turtle (*Eretmochelys imbricata*) is perhaps the most critically endangered of the marine turtles. It gets its name from the unique, hawk-like shape of its mouth. This turtle has long been hunted for its beautiful, layered shell, known as tortoiseshell. That's illegal now. Today, predators on land and at sea, coastal development, habitat degradation, trash and pollution, plus new ocean conditions due to climate change are challenging the survival of hawksbills around the world.

Please help us find 'Oli!

If you are lucky enough to spot a Hawaiian hawksbill, please send your photographs to Cheryl, who runs the statewide photo-ID catalog (1998-present). She'll compare the turtle's facial and flipper scale patterns, which are unique to each turtle, to identify which individual it is. If it's 'Oli (#MUI-27) or any of the other hawksbills we already know, we'll all be so happy to know that it's okay! If it's a new turtle to the catalog, you get to choose a name for it. All of this information will add to our understanding of this critically endangered species and aid in its protection. To learn more and join our Turtle Team please see:

www.HIhawksbills.org

We hope you enjoyed this true story about a little hawksbill sea turtle named 'Oli, and the community that cares so much about her and the ocean: Marjorie, Anita, Cheryl, Jake, Maile, George, Glynnis, Steve, and Esten.